Other books by Matthew Kaopio

Hawaiian Family Legends

Written in the Sky

Hawaiian Family Album

Hawaiian Family Album

Matthew Kaopio

Mutual Publishing

ISBN-10: 1-56647-870-7
ISBN-13: 978-1-56647-870-0

Library of Congress Cataloging-in-Publication Data

Kaopio, Matthew.
  Hawaiian family album / Matthew Kaopio.
      p. cm.
  ISBN-13: 978-1-56647-870-0 (alk. paper)
  ISBN-10: 1-56647-870-7 (alk. paper)

1. Legends--Hawaii. 2. Legends--Hawaii. I. Title.
  GR110.H38K36 2008
  398.209969--dc22

                                                2008023949

Design by Emily R. Lee

First Printing, July 2008

Mutual Publishing, LLC
1215 Center Street, Suite 210
Honolulu, Hawai'i 96816
Ph: 808-732-1709 / Fax: 808-734-4094
E-mail: info@mutualpublishing.com
www.mutualpublishing.com

Printed in Korea

Preface

My paternal grandmother Pearl Leilani White was born on January 19, 1917, to Annie Kane and Harry Lester White, Sr. the year Queen Lili'uokalani passed away. Her parents' common-law marriage was made legal later that year when Annie's husband Keao, who had been forcibly quarantined at Kalaupapa, died of leprosy. Originally from Maine, and having two children from a previous marriage, Grandpa White settled on Kaua'i with Annie, who had four previous pure Hawaiian children: Emogene, James, Annie, and Mary. From the second marriage came Eleanor, Lester, Grandma Pearl, Frances, George, and Blossom.

As a young child, Grandma was *hānai* (adopted) by her mother's younger half-sister, Polly Pauahi Nāka'ahiki. Auntie Polly lived in Kapahulu on Brokaw Street with her aging father, Nāka'ahiki Kāne, a *kahuna* who still practiced the ancient healing traditions. Honolulu in the 1920s was changing rapidly, but Grandma was raised speaking fluent Hawaiian. She lived with her adopted family until she moved back to Kaua'i with her birthparents at eight years old. It was the last time she would see "Tūtū-man" alive, although Auntie Polly lived until 1983, when she passed away at ninety-six.

Grandma lived a full life with seven children, twenty-three grandchildren, and several great-grandchildren. After contracting diabetes, she required long-term health care at Kaua'i's Wilcox Hospital. My sister Pauahi and I would visit, bringing her favorite dried shrimp and poi. Although Alzheimer's disease erased much of her short-term memory, her early childhood recollections were strong.

After the diving accident on August 17, 1994, which paralyzed me, I was flown to Queen's Medical Center in Honolulu for specialized care. Lying in my hospital bed I realized how lonely she must have felt. I spoke to her over the phone, but I really wanted to see my grandmother in person once more.

Months later, on a restless night in Kāne'ohe, I had a vision of a young woman's silhouette against a backdrop of flickering light. She had wavy long hair and an hourglass shape, but I could see through her like she was made of steam.

She moved her hand and placed it over my solar plexus. Three male figures appeared on the opposite side of the bed, placing their hands on hers one at a time. With each touch the glow grew brighter until the woman's features became clearer.

I was reminded of a black-and-white photograph Grandma kept of a 1930s hapa-haole hula girl. Suddenly the telephone rang, and I awoke staring at a blank wall. By the time my mom entered the room, I already knew Grandma had died.

Though she has reunited with her *kūpuna*, Grandma and her stories remain. We recorded her storytelling once with our cheap karaoke machine. My brothers and sisters listened to that cassette for hours, marveling at the mysticism of her *kahuna* upbringing.

Grandma passed away in June 1995 at the age of seventy-eight. She was buried next to her husband, Daniel Kaliʻa Kaopio, and their eldest son, Daniel Jr. Resting nearby are other extended family members in the same cemetery overlooking Kapaʻa town.

ʻAumakua still visit. My dad had several shark encounters while deep-sea diving, but always returned unharmed. And no matter if we lived in Kāneʻohe, Waialua, Kapaʻa, or ʻEwa Beach, owls still visit. Perhaps we sometimes need reminding that our ancestors are always with us.

Table of Contents

Prologue

"Grandma, what is ah-mah-koo-ah?" I asked her one Sunday while visiting her house after church. I knew if anybody could explain it to me, it was one of my grandparents, who were both fluent in the Hawaiian language.

"You mean 'aumakua?" she replied, standing at the sink, busy cleaning up after family brunch. "Where did you learn about that?"

"Some kids in school were talking about ah-mah-koo-ahs. What is that?" My grandmother stopped washing the dishes and turned to me, shutting off the water and drying her hands on the dishtowel hanging nearby.

"It's not ah-mah-koo-ah, it's 'aumakua."

"Sorry…'aumakua," I apologized, over-enunciating the word and waiting for her approval, which she was not giving. "My friend Stephen said his ah-mah-koo-ah was the shark and Jenny said hers was the owl."

"Really?" she said without smiling.

"Uh huh, and Brock told me his was the lizard. Is the lizard our ah-mah-koo-ah?" Grandma threw the towel down angrily.

"Don't you ever let me catch you saying that again, you hear me? We don't believe in those things anymore. We are Christian and there is only one God!"

"But Grandma…"

"I said I don't want to hear any more of this nonsense!" She grabbed the poi bowl and ran her finger around the edge, scraping the excess and licking it off her finger. Out of respect, I never brought up the subject again. I was only seven at the time and didn't understand what upset her so much. The other schoolkids' grandparents spoke freely about their family heritage, but for some reason mine felt ashamed.

But years later when Grandma's short-term memory began to decline, her inhibitions disappeared and the once-forbidden stories began to flow. It was as though she was reliving her childhood all over again.

One day I visited Grandma in her hospital room with my sister Pauahi and her baby.

"Who is this little blond-haired boy?" Grandma asked, pointing to my niece, sitting in my sister's lap.

"This isn't a boy, Grandma, this is Leilah, your great-granddaughter," I explained.

"Look at her blond hair. She looks like me when I was a baby. Did you know I was *hānai* to my auntie when I was that age?"

"Really?" I asked.

"Yes, I lived with Mama Polly and the old man Nāka'ahiki Kāne until I was eight years old."

"Eight years old?"

My grandmother stared off into space, allowing memories to flood her mind.

"Did I ever tell you about the time I almost died as a child?"

"No," I said, hoping for one of her stories.

"I was one rascal kid...real *kolohe*."

Family Photos

Grandma Pearl as a young hula girl

Grandma Pearl holding baby Annette

Hanai mother and daughter: Polly Nāka'ahiki and Pearl Leilani

Sister Annie – Earla

Grandma Pearl, Matthew, and sister Pauahi

Michael Nāka'ahiki

Mama Carol

Aunty Polly

Pearl & Daniel Kaopio, grandparents

Hard-head

While Polly Kalāhiki worked, her *hānai* hapa-haole daughter, Leilani, stayed home with Polly's elderly father, Nāka'ahiki Kāne. He was actually the brother of the little girl's biological grandfather, Sam Kāne. As was common in Hawaiian families, Nāka'ahiki, a widower, had married his brother's widow and they produced two more daughters: Polly, with the dark complexion; and light-skinned Ella. The girls were complete opposites, like Pele and Hi'iaka. Polly's older half-sister Annie had many children, so Leilani was *hānai* and taught the Hawaiian traditions.

It was Leilani's responsibility to make sure her grandfather had something to eat for lunch while her mother was gone for the day. One of her most important duties was to chew dried 'opae for her grandfather, who didn't have teeth. Because he loved the flavor of the dried shrimp with poi, the girl would soften the meat and place it in small clumps on his plate. When it was time to eat, he would put a clump of the savory mash in his mouth, roll it around on his tongue, and scoop up the poi with two fingers.

Occasionally the two took long walks together and he would either smoke his pipe or chew tobacco. Leilani was allowed to run ahead as he ambled casually behind. Outside there was a large mango tree which the kids loved to climb. Tūtū-man, as she affectionately called him, scolded his granddaughter when she climbed it, warning her that she could fall and get hurt if she wasn't careful. But like most kids, she didn't listen.

One particular hot summer day, Leilani saw a ripe red-and-orange mango dangling from the tree just beyond her reach. Imagining the sweet juices running down her throat while biting into the soft, orange flesh, she was immediately overcome with desire and could not resist picking it. Rather than getting the pole, she climbed onto the wooden fence nearby and stood as high as she could on tiptoes. The fruit was almost in her hand when her foot slipped and she fell off backward, slamming her head on a rock. Blood gushed everywhere. Her screams for help brought Tūtū-man hobbling quickly to Leilani's rescue.

"*Kēlā wahi keiki, ua kuli ka pepeiao!*" he scolded. Still conscious, she clung to him as her head became dizzy and everything started to spin. Her last memory before passing out was a burning at the back of her head where the old man spit a juicy wad of chewing tobacco directly on her open wound.

When Mama Polly returned from work, she was so upset that her shouting could be heard down the road. She scolded her father in Hawaiian, first for not watching the child, then for spitting tobacco on the open gash.

"*He aha kou mana'o? Paka nau?*"

"*E nānā aku 'oe i kona po'o,*" he said, telling his daughter to check the girl's head. "*Ua pau, ua oki!*"

"Pau? Where, show me!"

The old man pointed to the bedroom where his granddaughter had been sleeping all afternoon. Mama Polly entered the room, sat gently beside the girl, being careful not to wake her, and ran a hand over the back of her head. There, along with the crusty chewing tobacco and dried blood, was a slight depression where the wound had miraculously closed up completely. "What—how can?"

"See? I told you so," the old man called out to her from his seat at the dining room table. He opened his chewing tobacco pouch and tucked a large wad under his bottom lip. "Her just like you—Poʻopaʻakiki."

From that moment on Tūtū-man affectionately called his granddaughter "Poʻopaʻakiki" or "Hard-head."

Grandma's eyes began to water as her childhood memories took her to a time long past and soon to be forgotten.

"I still have the dent in the back of my skull. See?"

Grandma turned her head, lifted the white hair in the back, and let me trace my index finger along a slightly noticeable indentation.

"He must have been a great man," I said.

"I left them when I was eight years old. I wanted brothers and sisters. I never realized I would miss living with him and Mama Polly."

"Tell us more," my sister urged, her baby daughter acting like she understood.

"You know he said that every morning an angel would talk to him in the clouds and tell him what to expect later that day. And sure enough I would see people ride up on horseback. Even before they came he knew if he could help them or not because the angel already told him."

"A real angel?" Pauahi asked, looking skeptical.

"That man had visions…"

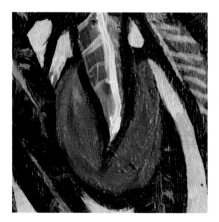

Grandfather's Morning

The old Hawaiian man got up before the rooster knew it was time to crow, while the pre-dawn sky was still dark as squid ink. He loved the early morning; everyone was still asleep and the silence was perfect for brooding and pondering about what the coming day held. He carefully poured water into the *pākini*, washing his hands and splashing the icy liquid on his face to jolt his senses. He sat back on his bed to slip on his favorite leather boots and, still shirtless, hobbled bow-legged out the front door.

For most of his adult life every morning began the same way. There were light chores to be done before the rest of the family awoke: the chickens needed feeding, there were eggs to collect, and the horse needed grooming. But before all of that, he took a seat in his favorite koa rocking chair on the front porch for a brief moment of reflection.

He pulled out his favorite pipe, which he had carved out of *liko lehua* wood. It was a hard, white wood with a sweet flavor. As always, he had to sneak a smoke before his daughter Polly woke up and gave him hell. This was his time: just him and the morning—and God.

The sun crawled groggily out of its earth blanket and splattered the still-starry sky with splotches of magenta and rose. The old man sat back, breathed a heavy sigh, and scanned the heavens for insight. To the east, near the morning star, a scarlet shark chased a legless chicken. Just as the predator was about to attack, the bird swerved and jabbed its beak into the shark's side. The shark's body dissipated, shattering into a school of baby fish, which the chicken devoured heartily. Interesting, the man thought. Someone will be arriving for relief from chickenpox. He'll be fine.

The man puffed softly and searched the skies again for anything else.

From the south, a bronze cumulus surged upward from its hiding place beneath the horizon: a wild horse released from bondage. Close behind loomed a sinister formation that remained shapeless. Puffing patiently on his pipe, Grandfather waited for a moment of clarity. The dark cloud became enraged and morphed into a huge three-horned dinosaur with its mouth gaping wide open. The horse darted frantically, but the lizard's teeth were locked on to its target. The horse reared up on its hind legs as the dragon's teeth sunk deeper. Legs flailed wildly but to no avail. The end was imminent. There was no hope for the victim. His illness was irreversible, and it was definitely his time to make preparations for his journey to the other side. Although the old man was used to divisions, he dreaded them.

Often people rode up on horseback, seeking a cure for some deadly illness or traumatic injury. Nāka'ahiki treated many Hawaiians who were dying in large numbers from unknown foreign diseases: they were either completely cured or given comfort for their ailments. If he could not

help them, which happened sometimes, he sent them home to make final arrangements.

Raised in the ancient traditions of prayers and chants by his father Naʻiliʻili, Nākaʻahiki remembered a time and place far different from the present. He was trained as a *kahuna kilokilo* to interpret the weather patterns and the portents of the heavens to gain spiritual instruction—a skill practiced by priests consecrated to the god Lonoʻōpuakau. As a *kahuna lāʻau lapaʻau*, Nākaʻahiki Kāne could ease the suffering of the afflicted and the dying with potions and prayers. Whenever possible, he gathered the necessary herbs and medicines to heal various ailments: the bitter *ʻuhaloa* root alleviated sore throat, *ʻolena* treated earaches, and there were multiple uses for *kukui*, *noni*, and aloe. But sadly, not all ailments could be treated.

Within his lifetime he'd witnessed the decimation of his people. A once vibrant and prosperous population had dwindled to only ten percent of its original size. The priests had long told of many changes to come and it saddened him to know that the ancient ways could all end with him.

He thought of his many grandchildren and great-grandchildren living throughout the Islands. Which one could he entrust with the knowledge? Would that power be abused? One more vision, he thought, and he began to chant an ancient prayer—one that he had placed in the back of his mind a long time ago and never thought of using again.

His voice began in a low rumble and ebbed and flowed like the surging tide. Words spilled from his mouth like watery poi through fingers, running into each other in an endless ribbon, only to be cut off and restarted by an occasional intake of air. Ancient, long-forgotten words of vast power strung together by one long, single breath. He raised his arms and the clouds sped up as the sun rose and set and rose again. Faster and faster the sun spun around the earth as if uncoiling a thread and binding everything around him.

Images flickered in his mind. What will come to pass? His heart raced as the random flashes congealed and he found the answer he was seeking. There they were, his seed, scattered across the Islands, thriving and growing against the repercussions of the ever-changing world. He saw educators, healers, artists, musicians, and peacemakers.

The vision was broken with the sound of horse hooves hitting pavement. He hadn't realized the sun had risen. "*Mai!*" he called out as he prepared to treat the visitor for his sickness.

Toa's Horse Troubles

James Keliʻikoa Silva, affectionately known as Toa, was Auntie Polly's son from her first husband. The boy loved his horse. ʻEleu was a sleek and powerful stallion that flew across land like God's fire. Every day after school, Toa brushed the shiny red coat, saddled up, and headed *mauka* for a ride along the Pali. As more automobiles frequented the city streets, fewer people rode on horseback. Nevertheless Toa went everywhere on his favorite horse. One day the worst happened: ʻEleu's hind leg got caught in a ditch and snapped in half. Imagine Toa's pain.

"Papa, please fix my horse's leg," Toa begged his grandfather.

"That horse … *pau* … *make*," the old man answered in broken English.

"*Aʻohe ona lua e like ai*," the boy pleaded, hoping that by speaking Hawaiian he could butter up the old man into performing a miracle.

"*Aʻohe ona ola!*" the man insisted, to deaf ears. "*Ua hala no!*"

"I know you can help if you like, old man!"

"Eeeeeaaaaah! Damm keed." Nākaʻahiki spat. He knew there was no convincing the boy. With pipe in hand he puffed slowly and racked his aging brains for the ancient recipe for mending broken bones.

It had been a while since he'd used his traditional knowledge. Usually a single gunshot solved this problem in an instant. But he knew the boy loved his horse too much to see it put down. Nākaʻahiki needed help, however. "*E Leilani,*" he shouted, "*hele mai!*"

Out came the spry, seven-year-old *hapa-haole* girl, Polly's *hānai* daughter and his *punahele*. "*E holoholo kāua, ʻohi lāʻau!*" The girl happily joined him to help gather herbs for the healing.

Retrieving his medicine bag and cowboy hat, Nākaʻahiki headed toward the Ala Wai with Leilani close behind. They want from Brokaw Street onto Kanaina and crossed busy Kapahulu Avenue when it was safe. Along the park fence grew a healthy patch of morning glory vines with delicate purple blossoms that seemed to bleed in the center.

"*Pōhuehue! E ʻohi!*" Nākaʻahiki ordered. Being left-handed, the girl instinctively reached out only to get a slap on her wrist. "*Ma ka ʻaoʻao ʻākau!*" he corrected, indicating his right hand.

She obeyed and wrapped the vine around her right fist as instructed. "*Maikaʻi,*" he said. "*Holo!*"

The two turned the corner onto Date Street, named for the many date palms that lined the sidewalk. The old man pointed at some fallen fruit under a tree. "*E kiʻi i kekahi!*"

Reaching for the big bunch, she was scolded once again. "*Ka mea liʻiliʻi,*" he quipped, "*o namunamu ka mea koe.*" She understood. If you gathered too much, the unused portion would grumble, leaving the medicine powerless. She reached for the smaller bunch.

Since the date fruit was edible as well as good for healing, they tasted some as they arrived at the bridge and spit the seeds into the canal below. This was an ideal spot to fish, catch prawns and crab, and gather seaweed. It was especially known for its *limu 'ele'ele*, a favorite of Auntie Polly's.

Along the water's edge grew patches of *laukahi*, needed to draw out infection. A broken leg got infected quickly and so in a clockwise motion, Leilani ripped off the soft leaves, careful not to pull out any roots. All the *laukahi* went into her grandfather's pouch.

By then, 1924, Nāka'ahiki felt that life in Honolulu was changing too rapidly: Chinese vendors hung roasted pork and duck in their windows, wealthy American tourists frolicked along the beaches, and U. S. sailors wandered around looking for relaxation. Only occasionally did another old-timer stop for a quick conversation in Hawaiian. Although the native language was still heard, it was becoming increasingly rare. It saddened Nāka'ahiki to think that the old traditions could be lost. He hoped that the girl would remember these times and perhaps share them with her own grandchildren.

They picked strawberry guavas and then headed home. It was afternoon by the time they returned to the dying horse and the pain-stricken Toa.

"*E ki'i i ka pale uluna!*" Nāka'ahiki ordered Leilani.

"*Pale uluna?*" she asked. "What dat?"

"*Ka mea…no kou po'o.*" He mimicked sleeping and pointed to his head. Entering the house, she returned with a cotton pillowcase from the closet.

Nāka'ahiki nodded, mixed the ingredients they had gathered with rock salt, and pounded everything with a polished stone. In a long rush of words she didn't understand, he occasionally breathed a loud "Ha!" over the sloppy mash. Still pounding, he sprinkled in tobacco and instructed Leilani to cut the material into long strips. "*E molina me ka lō'ihi.*"

"One last thing," he murmured, unbuttoning his pants to pull out what looked like a shriveled eggplant. Still mumbling, he let loose a heavy stream of urine over the pulp until only a few drops remained to mix into the mash.

The horse stood on three legs, the broken one raised. White bones jutted through the skin. 'Eleu's head and flanks were covered with patches of sweat. When Nāka'ahiki shoved the bones back into place, the horse let out a shrill whinny. The healer slapped on the poultice and wrapped it tightly with the white strips.

Auntie Polly screamed when she saw what her father had done to her brand-new pillowcases. He shrugged. "Five days," was all he said. In former times the severe wounds of warriors had been healed in a similar way.

Indeed, five days later it was like nothing had happened to 'Eleu. From his porch the old man puffed on his pipe, smiling contentedly as he watched Toa saddle up his beloved horse for a ride along the Pali. The boy was so excited he forgot to say thank you, then he turned and waved. "*Mahalo,*" his grandson shouted, "*mahalo*, Papa!"

The curious girl gazed out the window at her grandfather, who paced back and forth outside on the dusty road, smoking his pipe alone in the dark. He had on his best shirt, musk cologne, and his hair was combed neatly. Obviously he waited to meet someone very important.

"*E Mā*," she asked her *hanai* mother, "*e aha ana ʻo Tūtū kāne ma waho?*"

"*Tsā, mai niele ʻoe!*" Polly scolded, saying not to be so nosy.

"*No ke aha ʻo ia e kali nei?*" Leilani repeated, still waiting for an answer.

"*He aha kaʻu i ʻolelo ai?*" Polly pulled her daughter away from the windowsill, giving her a soft pat on the behind. "*Mai niele ʻoe!*" The girl obeyed but returned to the window later. Her grandfather was gone.

A week passed and Leilani noticed that on certain nights her grandfather went wandering in the dark, only to return just before sunrise. She kept asking her mother, "*E aha ana ʻo Tūtū kāne ma waho?*"

Finally Polly gave in to her daughter's persistent questioning and reluctantly told her about Nākaʻahiki Kāne's night activities. "You not going believe me, but he waiting for his sweetheart."

"Hah? How can? He's too old!"

"But to his sweetheart, he is much younger." Polly looked around and spoke in Hawaiian to make sure no neighbor could understand their conversation. "*ʻO Pele kāna wahine o ka pō.*"

"*O ia kā?*" Leilani exclaimed in disbelief. Pele was the old man's lover? It seemed impossible because their family lived on Oʻahu, far away from the volcano. "*Pehea kēlā? Aia ʻo Pele e noho nei ma Hawaiʻi. Kaʻawale kēlā ʻāina, a mamao loa aku.*"

"*Holo maila ka wahine o ka lua ma kona lio ahi wela, a lele ma luna o ke kai a hiki i Oʻahu, a kiʻi ʻia kou Tūtū kāne, a hoʻi akula i Hawaiʻi lā.*"

She rode across the ocean on a horse of fire. It all seemed incredible to Leilani. "*I hea lāua e hele ai?*" she asked, wondering where the couple could possibly go, knowing that her grandfather would burn to a crisp if he entered the volcano. "*ʻAʻole hiki iā Tūtū kāne ke komo i loko o ka lua pele!*"

"*Ae, hiki nō ke komo!*" Polly corrected her.

"*Pehea lā ʻo ia e hana ai?*" The girl was confused to hear that he was an invited guest.

"*Ke heleleʻi ʻo Pele,*" her mother explained, "*oluʻolu ka pele, ʻaʻohe wela. Hoʻokau ʻo Tūtū kāne kona wāwae i loko o ka helehelena, a pēlā nō ʻo ia e komo ai i ka lua pele.*"

Leilani tried to envision her mother's description of the old man stepping into the goddess's footprints, where the lava would cool enough for him to enter safely. *Ua pau ke ahi i kona helehelena.* The fire went out in Pele's footsteps. It seemed like a clever solution. "*A pau ka hana, hoʻi maila i ke kakahiaka aʻe?*" she asked, thinking that her Tūtū man always returned the following morning.

"*Pololei nō!*" Polly exclaimed. Of course, that's how it goes.

Leilani accused her mother of joking. "*Kūpaianaha! Hoʻopunipuni ʻoe.*"

"*He ʻoiaʻiʻo nō, hoʻohiki au,*" Polly promised, crossing her heart. "*No ia kumu au i kapa ʻia ai ka inoa ʻo Pauahi.*"

From her hospital bed Grandma told exactly the same story to my sister Pauahi and me when we visited her with baby Leilah. "And that is why," Grandma concluded, "Mama Polly was named Pauahi, because of the fire goddess."

"So that's also the meaning of my name?" my sister asked. Her daughter Leilah-Irene Pauahi Cooper sat contentedly in her lap.

Grandma smiled patiently, as if used to explaining complicated family relationships. "Yes, Pauahi was my Mama's true name. Her English name was Polly. Even my sister Blossom was named after her…"

"Yeah," remarked my sister, "so is our cousin, Debra."

"Yes. *Ua pau ke ahi.* The fire ended."

"I thought Elzy called me Bernicia Pauahi after Princess Bernice Pauahi Bishop because she was going to Kamehameha Schools."

"Yes. But Pauahi is also our family's name."

We sat quietly, feeling all those relationships binding together five generations of Hawaiian women with a sacred name of great strength.

The Pū'olo

"I lived with my Aunt until I was eight years old." Grandma said, not realizing she was repeating herself. "Then I asked if I could move back with my birth parents on Kaua'i."

"Yes, Grandma, you told us that." I gently combed her white hair as she spoke. Pauahi and her baby listened quietly.

"Growing up in Kapahulu," Grandma went on, "I was an only child and I wanted brothers and sisters. Soon after I went to Kaua'i, Nāka'ahiki Kāne passed away in Honolulu. All his knowledge of the old craft died with him. Most of my family became Mormon converts so nobody wanted to carry on the old Hawaiian traditions. The Church was against those practices—you know, you could get excommunicated if you got caught doing that."

Grandma eyed me as though she would reveal something exciting. "While making funeral arrangements, Mama Polly was going through her father's things and she found his medicine bag: the same one he used to take with him when gathering herbs. He never showed me what was inside. But I remember seeing him talking to it and stroking it like it was a living person. I just thought he was getting dementia in his old age. But Mama Polly found something inside that frightened her."

"What was it?" I asked.

"She found one *pū'olo*. It's a small bundle made of *kapa* from the *wauke* plant. The ancient Hawaiians used to pound the bark for clothing. The men would tie it into a *malo*, and women would wear it as a *pā'ū* skirt. Inside this *pū'olo* were human teeth, bones, hair…"

"Hair? Teeth and bones?" my sister repeated, very interested. "From where?"

"I don't know. But in the olden days, people doing black magic would collect parts of a dead person to do their bidding. The old-timers call it *'anā'anā*. If a *kahuna* got a hold of someone's bones, especially a chief's, who knows what they could do? That's why burials were kept secret—to prevent the soul of the loved one from becoming *unihipili*."

"Uni—he…what?" Pauahi stared.

Grandma put her finger to her lips. "Never mind. Better you don't know the word. But what it means is that the *'uhane* becomes a slave under the *kahuna's* control. The *kahuna* can attack anybody he wants, as long as he gets something belonging to the victim: panties from the clothesline, hair, a photograph, even a fingernail…"

"Is that why we don't clip our fingernails at night?" my sister interrupted.

"Yes! Cutting them at night is forbidden. I always flush mine down the toilet."

"So that's why you always clean the hairbrush?" I asked, still combing her hair. She was almost obsessive about that.

"And always remember to take the clothes off the line before dark," Pauahi added. "Remember what happened to Papa when his shirt was stolen off the line?"

"He had human bite marks all over his body," I said. The memory of it made me shudder.

"Wait." My sister turned to Grandma. "So what ever happened to the bundle?"

"Oh yes, I almost forgot about the bundle! Well, Mama Polly tried to get rid of it, but no matter what she did it would come back. It was as if it needed somebody to take care of it. My mother had an idea: she thought if she could take it with her on the ship, maybe she could throw it out to sea. Back then we didn't have airplanes; we traveled interisland by boat. So she hid the bundle in the pocket of her dress and got on the ship. But before they could leave the dock, something strange happened."

"What?" Pauahi demanded. Even her baby seemed intrigued by the story.

"The water level rose all the way to the edge of the boat, almost spilling over onto the deck. It was like there was something heavy keeping the boat from floating. Of course, everyone panicked. The captain, who was Hawaiian, knew something was wrong. He asked every person if they had any idea why it was happening. My mother knew that it was the bundle she was carrying that was causing all this, but she did not say a word. Finally the captain ordered everyone off the boat. Things went back to normal. Then everyone was allowed back one by one. As soon as my mother set foot on deck, the water level rose again. The captain knew it was my mother and she was told to leave."

"Then what?" my sister and I asked unison.

"That's when she called a family meeting. This was too big for her to solve on her own. After many hours it was finally settled: the *pū'olo* had to be destroyed. The only one willing to do it was one of my uncles. He decided to burn it in the backyard."

Grandma sat up as though recalling the scene. "As soon as he tossed the bundle into the fire, there was a burst of blue flame and a loud scream like a crying baby. It shot straight up into the sky, forming a gigantic blue fireball, and headed out to sea, bouncing on the ocean, never to be seen again."

"How freaky," my sister whispered, her eyes bulging.

"And my story's not over yet. That same uncle…sugars, I forgot his name but I remember he was half Hawaiian-half popolo…he became completely blind after that and soon died a miserable death. Some say it was diabetes. I think it's because he wasn't supposed to handle that responsibility. But there was no other choice. As long as that *pū'olo* existed without a proper caretaker, it would feed on the souls of everyone around it. You can call it superstition if you like, but nothing good ever came out of that *'anā'anā* stuff."

Pauahi and I traded a long look as if to say we would not forget the story. Grandma asked for the brush when I finished with her hair and she picked out every last strand until the bristles were clean.

The Pueo

could tell all this family talk made my sister eager for more. She had the same look on her face when she was ready for a second serving at family lūʻaus.

"Grandma," Pauahi asked, "do you know if the owl is our ʻaumakua?"

"What you think?" my grandmother asked her right back.

"What do you mean?" Now my sister looked confused.

"Have you ever seen one show up when you needed help?"

Pauahi didn't reply and I thought back to the time both of us went hunting up in Kōkeʻe with my Dad. He drove his blue Chevy Blazer like we were flying down the winding roads. As we came around a bend a large brown blur rushed from the mountainside on the left, just missed the windshield, and landed on a tree on the opposite side of the road. Startled, my Dad swerved and narrowly avoided a huge truck speeding in our direction. It was only a split-second but I clearly remembered staring out my passenger window to see the owl glare at me.

"Actually, yes," I said.

Grandma tipped up her chin. "Pueo are definitely our family guardians."

She went on to explain that owls seemed to show up in times of great danger or during special occasions. The owl might be white, actually the newly introduced kind, but most times it was the brown ones, native to the Islands and here before our ancestors arrived.

"So often my family was saved by pueo." After a thoughtful pause she gave an example:

"One night, Mama Polly's husband came home drunk. She was upset because he spent almost his whole paycheck at the bars and they began arguing. And as usual, he started to beat her. Frightened, she ran outside with her lip all bloody. Her husband shouted threats. She could hardly see in the dark and called for help, but the next house was too far away for anybody to hear. The thought of her husband's heavy fists made her panic.

"Just then Mama Polly spotted one small owl sitting on a fencepost, staring with big round yellow-ringed eyes. Pueo twisted its head, spread its wings, and flew a short distance onto the next fencepost. It turned to her again, as if trying to get her attention, and hopped onto the next fencepost. This seemed unusual, but for some reason Mama Polly knew she should follow. Together they went off quietly in the dark. That owl took her to a safe place where the drunkard couldn't find her.

"The next morning Mama Polly returned home. Her husband had sobered and forgotten about what happened the night before. Her face was all bruised but he wouldn't apologize. Well, Mama Polly had put up with that bull *kiʻo* long enough! Later that day she threw out all his things and

made him sit on the curb in the rain. Soon after that, they were divorced."

Grandma stopped speaking and smiled to herself, enjoying the memory of a strong wahine.

"Did pueo ever help you?" I asked.

For a moment Grandma was silent. Then she spoke again.

"When I was a little girl, I just moved back to Kaua'i with my family. My mother Annie wanted to go to a family party a few towns away. Back then, my haole father drove one of those Ford Model Ts, the kind you crank in the front to jumpstart. With my mother in the back seat, we drove until it started to rain. It was getting dark and raining so hard you could barely see anything in front. Mind you, this was before the invention of the automatic windshield wiper. Back then you had to move the wiper back and forth by hand. I was in the front passenger seat, moving the lever back and forth. My hand was getting sore. But no matter how fast it cranked, the water poured over the glass like a waterfall.

"All of a sudden a big bird came down out of nowhere. It flew directly at the windshield and flapped its wings against the glass. I kid you not! The wings hit the glass: 'Tap, tap, tap!'

"Well, I remember the story told to me by Mama Polly and I knew something wasn't right. My father wanted to keep going but the farther we went the more the brown bird flew in front of us, hitting its wings harder against the glass. My mother was raised in the Hawaiian traditions like me, and from the back seat she said, 'Eh, I think this is a sign of danger. We better turn around now!'

"My haole father had learned never to question Hawaiian beliefs. Right then and there he turned the Model T around. We went straight home and missed the party.

"Sure enough, we found out the next morning that the rain had been so heavy it caused the river to overflow and the bridge got washed away. Who knows what would have happened if we never turn around? Maybe we would have all died if the owl hadn't warned us."

Thoughtfully Grandma nodded. "There were many times throughout my life when I saw pueo face-to-face. The old-timers say an owl flying on the right side of your car is a good sign. But if you see it on your left, then be careful because that is a sign of danger."

I recalled my own experience, how the owl flew in front of our Chevy Blazer windshield from the mountainside on the left. My sister remembered the incident clearly, so I told the story to our grandmother.

Grandma smiled and nodded again, this time knowingly. "I need to have a word with my son about his reckless driving..."

Kāne-o-kekai: Man of the Sea

This time Grandma started talking without any coaxing from us. "*Pueo*," she said, "wasn't the only form our family guardians took. There were other animals…

"Mama Polly used to go down to the beach to pick *'opihi* and *limu*, well past her golden years. Did I mention she lived to be ninety-six? She always wanted to reach one hundred, but she missed it by four years. I visited her in Kapahulu where she lived in the same house I grew up in until the 1970s when she lived with Pauahi Freitas.

"For my *hānai* mother, the ocean provided a rich banquet of delicacies. My love for seafood came from living with her and the old man, Nāka'ahiki Kāne. Because Tūtū-man had no teeth, my mother prepared *i'a maka* (raw fish) *lomilomi* style. That's when you mash it up with your fingers. He loved them all: *pāpa'i* and *'a'ama* (crabs), *wana* (sea urchin), *loli* (sea cucumber), even *he'e* (octopus). My favorite was *hā'uke'uke*, fresh off the rocks. I could eat a whole bucketful myself until my hands ran purple from all the juices. *Hū ka 'ono!*

"That woman knew all the ideal places to find the best seaweed. You name it: *limu kohu, lipoa, wāwae 'iole,* and *'ele'ele*. Proper gathering technique meant softly raking the bed with your fingers, being careful not to remove the roots from the reef. Careless pickers sometimes ripped out whole plants, sand and all, wiping out future generations of seaweed.

"There was also a proper way to pick *'opihi*. It required a skilled hand and was almost an art form. The little creatures thrive on seaweed that grows on the black rocks facing the ocean. In between wave sets *'opihi* relax and they can be easily gathered with a quick slice of the knife. But if they sense the slightest movement they cling tightly, and cannot be pried from the rock no matter what.

"In stormy weather, 'opihi picking is extremely dangerous. When the water is rough you have to watch the waves all the time. Never turn your back to the ocean. Just one strong wave can slam you against sharp rocks, or worse, sweep you out to sea. *'Opihi* pickers can get cut or knocked unconscious and drown.

"One day Mama Polly was gathering *hā'uke'uke* and *wana*. She saw a big bunch of *'opihi* as large as the palm of her hand. They faced the ocean on a slippery rock that was difficult to reach. She climbed down. Even with years of experience, just as she was picking one the size of a small coconut, a huge wave came crashing into her. Nothing could have prepared her for what happened next: after the first wave there was another and another, until her own hands lost their grip on the rocks and she was swept out to sea.

"Hitting and scraping on boulders and coral, her cut hands and feet bloodied the blue water. The undertow pulled at her, and she struggled to keep her face above the surface. Her flower-print *mu'umu'u* tangled in her legs. The net bag of

limu and *'opihi* weighed her down. She sank, gasping for air, as the ocean dragged her farther from shore. Several times she managed to kick upward and capture small bubbles of air. She resisted the impulse to fight the current and tire herself out. As long she could she held her breath and rode the flow until the undertow lost strength way out at sea.

"Aue! Now what? Too far away for anybody to see her or hear her shouting.

"In the deep blue water Mama Polly kicked her tired legs once again and kept her head above the surface. She gasped for air but only gulped the sandy water. Then she remembered her father saying that if she were ever at sea and needed help, all she had to do was call on their family guardian. She struggled once again for breath and managed to cough out a name: 'Kāne-o-kekai!'

"Just then a dark shadow appeared from nowhere. A large figure came up underneath her, lifting her high enough out of the water to cough again and fill her lungs with air. Breathing raggedly, her hands touched something rough like sandpaper. She stared down and realized that she was holding on to the dorsal fin of a great white shark. *Mano.* Man of the sea.

"The shark swam swiftly toward land as Mama Polly held on tight. When they came close to shore the shark gave one quick snap of its tail and my mother was flung onto dry sand. Her net bag flopped beside her. She stood up on the beach, thanking her guardian of the sea for saving her life.

"Ha'alele 'o Pele no ka 'āina ma lalo,
Kūkamakaia 'o Nāmaka-o-Kaha'i!
No'eau ka hoe a Kamohoali'i,
A pae i uka i ke one malo'o!"

For a moment we were all silent, a dream to see: waves, sand, and the shark disappearing. Mama Polly bloody, but alive.

"Wasn't she scared?" my sister asked.

"Of course," our grandmother replied, "she told me she almost peed her pants!" We all laughed until we were gasping.

"Grandma," I asked once we caught our breaths, "was this Kāne-o-kekai related to us because our family name is Kāne?"

She fixed me with a look. "Remember when I told you that our family guardian is Pele?" Pauahi and I both nodded our heads. "Well, her older sister was the ocean goddess, Nāmaka-o-Kaha'i. The legend goes that Pele offended her sister and had to leave her home in Polapola. Pele escaped to Hawai'i with the help of her older brother, the shark god Kamohoali'i. The ocean goddess chased her all the way to Hawai'i and even till today they still fight one another. Water and fire. Fire and water. But if you ever find yourself out at sea and you need help, just call Kāne-o-kekai."

My sister and I turned to each other at the same time with the same expression as if she were crazy.

"Nevermind."

Beware the Moʻo

"**G**randma, remember when I was in the second grade and I wanted to know about the *moʻo*? I asked her. "Why did you get mad at me?"

My niece was twisting around in my sister's lap so Pauahi took her for a walk around the hospital wing. But Pauahi left with a look of regret as if she knew she would be missing a good story.

"Oh yes," our grandmother murmured to me, "the lizard."

"Lots of people say the lizard is their family guardian."

"Well, for my family it's the enemy. Listen to this: My mother Annie was pregnant and close to childbirth. One night she was sitting in her bedroom and a black lizard crawled through a crack in the wall. It slithered its body over until it was only inches away from her face. Well, my mother was scared so she tried to shoo it away. But the lizard never moved. She yelled and hit the wall. That darned lizard came closer and started sticking its tongue at her. Yap, yap, yap, just like this!" Grandma darted her tongue rapidly in and out. I laughed at the expressions she made.

"You laugh, but it wasn't funny to her. She screamed bloody murder and jumped from one bed to the other (you know, they had twin beds back then instead of a king-size). Anyway, would you know that gunfunnit buggah chased her? Yes! That thing ran up the wall, across the ceiling, and down the other side next to her on the other twin bed."

"What did she do?"

"She was so scared she jumped back to the other bed. The lizard followed her again and she had a miscarriage, right there."

"Oh, I'm sorry." I wasn't laughing anymore.

"And would you know? That very thing happened to her twice!"

"Miscarried two times? You mean two babies died?"

"Yes! That's why I was afraid when your mother screamed that a lizard jumped on her stomach in the shower. I think she was pregnant with you."

"Mom told me about that."

When my parents were newlyweds they lived with Grandma and Grandpa Kaopio on their Hawaiian homestead land in Waimānalo. Dad went to Vietnam in 1968 with the Navy and he was away a lot. One day Mom was taking a bath when a lizard jumped from the wall and landed on her big belly. Startled, she tried to brush it away but the creature did not move. She screamed for help and Grandma came in, yelling something at it in Hawaiian. Finally the lizard ran away and Grandma told her if that ever happened again, not to get excited or she could lose the baby.

Grandma eyed me. "Well, she didn't lose you. Nobody knows for sure why *hapai* women in our family had bad luck with lizards. My mother was pure Hawaiian and superstitious. She thinks maybe we were cursed."

Down the hall Pauahi's footsteps came closer. Quickly I said to Grandma, "When I was a kid I heard if you smashed lizard eggs, the mother got revenge by coming to your house and sticking her tail in your ear."

"Not," my sister said, returning to take a seat with the baby asleep on her shoulder. "If the tail breaks off, cover your ears 'cause going inside and make you deaf!"

Grandma laughed. "Yes, I heard of both. But our family quarrel goes way back to Pele." We raised our eyebrows, encouraging her to go on. "Well, long ago in ancient times, a member of the Pele family offended the mo'o."

"Really," my sister said. "I thought they were related."

"No," Grandma corrected her. "Remember the story of Hi'iaka's voyage from Halema'uma'u to Kaua'i to bring back Pele's husband, Lohi'au?"

"No," Pauahi said, although I knew the story pretty well.

"When Pele's youngest sister left her volcano home, she encountered danger along the way. In several 'ahupua'a, there were evil spirits making trouble for unsuspecting travelers and commoners. Some of them were *mo'o*—not the small kine like we get today, but big, scary buggahs."

"You mean like alligators?" Pauahi giggled.

"Eh, no laugh," Grandma warned. "Bigger than alligators. Some were yellow-green, but the scarier ones were dark. Black. Sometimes they would hide in water ditches, or freshwater ponds where you cannot see the bottom. Or they lived in caves. Up Hā'ena get plenty caves where people swear they saw strange things."

Growing up on Kaua'i, it was common knowledge not to venture alone in the deep caverns around Hanalei. A few people tried, including a science teacher who entered the wet cave in a boat with a rope attached. Somehow the line was severed and the man was never heard from again. The locals insisted it was a *mo'o* that got him.

"How come nobody caught one yet?" My sister was always the skeptic.

"Because Hi'iaka slaughtered most of them. There was Pana'ewa, Mokoli'i…oh sugars, so much I forget. But if you don't believe me, go see for yourself. Don't say I didn't warn you. I no make up these stories, I tell you what I know. And I wouldn't fut around with Hawaiian superstitions."

Maybe I should have listened. Weeks later, I went to Waipāhe'e, a well-known *mo'o* dwelling, and nearly died in the diving accident that made me paralyzed today. And three years later, in 1997, a good friend of mine drowned there. Where do you draw the line between ancient wisdom and old wives' tales? Whether the stories were real, or merely concocted to prevent tragedy from happening, no one can say. But as long as people continue to believe, there is little difference between a harmless-looking gecko and a man-eating water dragon.

Tūtū Pele at the Crater

I couldn't help but stare at Grandma with disbelief. She was talking as if these characters from folktales were actual people.

"You know I saw her with my own eyes?" Grandma said, as if reading my thoughts.

"Who?" I asked.

"*Ka wahine o ka lua,*" she mentioned to me, happy that one of her grandchildren decided to learn to speak Hawaiian language in college.

"*'O wai lā? Ka wahine?*"

"This story is true," she explained, reverting to English. "I cross my heart..."

Once again she settled back to speak uninterrupted. I leaned forward and felt like both of us sensed time was short.

"I took a trip to the Big Island in the 1960s with my sisters. My half-sister Mary, who lived up Big Island, just passed away so we went for her funeral. While we were there we heard that Pele just erupted—she was asleep for a while, but there was an earthquake and once again the lava was flowing. A group of us wanted to rent a van to drive up the crater. It was my first time going, so I was real excited. I remembered all my small-kid time stories of Tūtū-man at the *lua pele* long ago. I felt like he was with me and I was seeing one long-lost relative. We went

go nighttime fo' see the glow, because we heard was much nicer after sunset.

"There I was at the edge of the crater—*hu*, the rim stretched out for miles. I looked across. Just then the wind blew and a flame leaped up out of the volcano. It was so clear to me—like a woman riding a fiery horse. She held on tight to the horse's mane with one hand and waved with the other, galloping along the edge. I turned to my mother to see if she saw the vision, but she was crying softly, mumbling something in Hawaiian.

"I tried to take pictures with my Kodak camera but was too late—the vision was gone in seconds. No one else saw the woman on horseback, but I swear it happened. I looked down into the lava, and I saw a woman's face. Inside her flowing hair was the eight Hawaiian islands. I pointed it out to everybody, and they all saw it. She showed herself to me. That's how I knew Mama Polly's stories were real. Pele was alive! I took as many pictures as my camera could. When it was time to go, we said our 'Aloha.'

"Everybody was tired so we slept on the way back. But so was the driver—he fell asleep at the wheel. All I remember was waking up to a loud 'thump!' When I looked out the window I saw only pitch black. Then I noticed the road was above eye level. The van went off the road and fell into a ditch. Can you believe we

didn't roll over? We landed on all four tires! Somebody or something was watching over us that night. I don't know if it was a guardian angel, or God, or the volcano goddess. But none of us was harmed—everybody came out without a scratch.

"We caught ride into town on one early-morning delivery truck. It wasn't until I got off that I remembered I forgot the camera. When the van was towed back to the rental car place, I wen' go look for 'em but was gone. I was so upset that I lost those pictures. But maybe that's why we got into the accident—we were not meant to keep those pictures."

Pōhaku

"Grandma, what about stones?" my sister spoke up, making sure to get her chance to ask questions. "Is it bad luck to gather stones?"

"People say you shouldn't take home rocks," I chimed in, curious for her opinion.

"Well, it all depends."

Pauahi frowned. "What do you mean?"

"Stones have *mana*, there's no denying that. Didn't you hear about the stones of Wailua River Valley?

"Long ago, Wailua Valley was home to the highest-ranking chiefs. They were treated like gods. The birthing place was so sacred that anyone born would become very powerful. That is why the entire *'ahupua'a* division, from mountain to sea, was off limits. If a pregnant commoner had a son while leaning against that rock, he could overthrow the reigning chief. That's how special that stone was."

"That's next to the *piko* rock before going up Wailua Homestead Road, right?" I asked, remembering several past school excursions. "The one with the cracks where the chiefs placed their belly buttons?"

Grandma nodded. "Yes, the *piko* represented a person's connection to the *makua*. To the Hawaiians, that body part was sacred and held a person's power. Some chiefs buried theirs and planted trees on top, but some hid them deep inside the rock's crevice."

"And if a rat stole it, the baby would grow up to be a thief," I reminded her.

"That's what people say. I guess it wouldn't be a good thing if a chief stole from his people," Grandma answered.

"But do rocks have spirits?" Pauahi questioned, unsatisfied with the answer.

"Well, there are two large rocks by the Wailua River. Some say they rolled across the ocean floor from Kahiki. Others say a sister sits on the cliff overlooking her brother who died after jumping into the river below. That is the rock the riverboats have to go around when they go up Fern Grotto."

"Didn't the rock bleed when some people drilled a hole inside to move it with a crane?" I asked, remembering the riverboat captain's tales.

"I heard somebody played a hoax using pig's blood," Grandma mentioned.

"No," Pauahi insisted. "Dad found rocks up in Hanakāpi'ai he said called to him."

"Really?" Grandma asked, intrigued.

I explained to her about the smooth pointed rock we carried home from one of our Nā Pali camping trips. Every summer since I was thirteen, my dad would take us hiking along the Kalalau trail. Spying a pyramidal blue stone among the rubble, Dad decided to keep it. When we returned home, he tried to write the date on it with a permanent pen, but the writing disappeared the following morn-

ing. That same stone is still being used as a doorstop for the front entrance at our house.

"Our friends teased us and said we'd get punished," Pauahi said.

"Oh, like taking lava rock from the volcano?" Grandma said with a growing smile.

"Yes! Is it true?"

"Honestly," Grandma laughed, "it depends on what you believe."

"I don't understand," my sister said with frustration.

Grandma explained that the rock superstition was invented by a non-Hawaiian park ranger who wanted to prevent erosion and vandalism from tourists. Those believing the myth blame their troubles on the stone. But Hawaiians were Stone Age people who depended on stones for daily living. Certain rocks were better for cooking in the underground *imu*, while others made strong adzes for carving canoes.

"If nobody gathered stones, how could anyone live?" Grandma said, with a chuckle.

"So that's just superstition?" Pauahi exclaimed with a look of relief.

"Rocks are nothing but small bits of broken down volcanoes. And those bits will only end up turning into smaller bits, until you have nothing left but dirt. Those rocks were there way before any of us were born, and they will be around long after we're gone."

"Wait till I tell 'em they wrong," my sister promised.

Grandma shook her head, pointing her finger to her lips with a soft "shhh." "Let them believe whatever they want."

A Blessed Birth

soaked in all of Grandma's words and tried to apply them to specific incidents in my own life. Seeing Pauahi's daughter Leilah reminded me of the day she was born.

"Grandma," I asked during a brief moment of silence. "Is it a good thing to see an owl when someone is giving birth?"

"Sometimes there were signs in the heavens or an appearance of 'aumakua, especially during the birth of the chief," Grandma said.

"Like rainbows?" my sister asked as her baby daughter climbed down from her lap.

"Of course! The arching *pi'o* rainbow, as in the name *Kapi'olani*, signaled a chief of the highest *kapu*. Usually *kahuna kilo lani* would scan the heavens. The *'onohi* rainbow clouds were very special. *Kahuna mo'oku'auhau* recited the child's genealogy while the mother was in labor so the child would be linked to the ancestors."

"That's just like the night Leilah was born," I told them as my mind recalled the previous year when I witnessed the birth of my parents' first grandchild.

It was December 19, 1992, and my sister Pauahi had been in labor at Wilcox Hospital all night. The baby was actually due a week before. But because Pauahi's water hadn't broken yet, the midwife encouraged her to walk around so that she could get dilated. She insisted on having a natural birth rather than cesarean, so Pauahi refused pain medicine.

Everyone had placed bets on the baby's projected due date. I already lost with December 14, and it looked like my cousin Elea was going to win for predicting it on her own birthday. It was in March at Grandpa Nāihe's funeral when my sister revealed she was pregnant.

Auntie Keala, who was riding with me to the hospital, spotted the owl flying *mauka* on the right side of our car. My father's sister became deaf when she contracted German measles as a young child, but her vision remained sharp. Mumbling loudly and signing too rapidly for me to read and drive, she pointed to a brown silhouette too large to be a pigeon. I instinctively glanced to my left at the sunrise, admiring the faint rainbow amidst the rose, orange, and yellow clouds.

Mom had been with Pauahi all night and needed to go home to get refreshed. Just as we arrived, Mom rushed home to shower and get ready for the baby's arrival. Before leaving the house she searched for some Hawaiian cassette tapes to play soothing music on the delivery room's stereo. Finding a blank one entitled "Honolulu City Lights," she headed back to the hospital in barely under an hour.

By this time Pauahi was exhausted. Her membrane had to be broken manually and she was still not dilating. That's

when the midwife realized the infant needed to be rotated in the womb. Enduring the pain the best she could, my sister got on all fours while the midwife massaged her belly to move the baby into proper birthing position. Pauahi lay back down, placed her feet in the stirrups, and began to push. Just as the baby's head was emerging, the music stopped and a man's voice was heard speaking.

In a soft tone the man recounted his family's history to the chiefs of Kohala. He remembered being told by his grandfather, James Kamaka Nāihe, about his ancestor Nāihe, a high chief and supporter of King Kamehameha, who is buried in the Kalākaua mausoleum beside his wife, Kapiʻolani. James Kamaka Nāihe was described as a handsome man who walked with bowed legs from years of horse riding. He was a sheriff and community leader. As a young man, he served his people in kingdom affairs as a representative to the House of Commons for North Kona.

The man described his boyhood in Kohala, the oldest son of Henry Moaʻe Nāihe and Ah Lan Kupukaʻa Ah Sam. His older brother Henry had been shot accidentally by an uncle while playing "cowboys and Indians" with a handgun. This led the family to believe the name Moaʻe was cursed, since every child given that name died prematurely.

At twelve years old the man lied about his age so he could work on a cattle ranch. When he reached adulthood he joined the military and was stationed in Germany, where he fathered a child with a French woman. He eventually returned to Hilo where he married Irene Kahalelaukoa Baker. After his wife's death from uterine cancer in 1965, he married her younger sister and raised a total of thirteen children.

Mom immediately recognized her father's voice over the speakers. Dying from a brain tumor nine months earlier, Edward Nāihe Sr. visited his relatives throughout the Islands in a final attempt to tie up loose ends. On one particular evening, while he was sharing some of his childhood memories, my mom inserted a blank cassette tape into the karaoke machine and handed him the microphone, hoping to capture his biography. Although she was successful, the tape went missing soon after. Apparently my sister's boyfriend Andy found the tape and recorded music on it, thinking it was blank.

My niece Leilah-Irene Pauahi Cooper had part of her genealogy recited at the precise moment she entered the world. Some people would think this incident was insignificant, but for those in the room we knew our ancestors were present.

Grandma's eyes were filled with tears as Pauahi confirmed the truth of my story.

"I wasn't aware that happened," Grandma said as my sister hugged her and dabbed her eyes with a tissue. "I guess even an old woman can learn from her grandchildren."

"So, was that an ʻaumakua experience?" my sister asked.

"Absolutely," she explained. "People mistake ʻaumakua as animals, but that's only the forms the ancestors take when they come back. They can be clouds, a song on the radio, even a whiff of perfume. That cassette tape showing up at that moment doesn't sound like a coincidence to me."

About the Author

Matthew Kaopio began his career as a mouth-brush artist and writer while going through rehabilitation after a 1994 diving accident that left him a quadriplegic. He is the author of *Hawaiian Family Legends* and *Written in the Sky*. He has a BA in Hawaiian/Pacific studies and an MA in Pacific Island studies. In March 2004, he was accepted into the Association of Mouth and Foot Painting Artists, a for-profit company that supports hundreds of disabled artists around the world.